T3-BNX-022

Gift
of
Margaret Bradford

EDGES

EDGES

By

Virginia Clark Clarkson

THE GOLDEN QUILL PRESS
Publishers
Francestown   New Hampshire

Library of Congress Catalog Card Number 86-81282

ISBN 0-8233-0423-X

Published in the United States of America

Dedicated to my friend-teachers
who encouraged writers and demonstrated
the discipline required to be one:
Winthrop Palmer and Sally Ronsheim.

CONTENTS

New Hampshire

Sailing

East Hampton

NEW HAMPSHIRE

EARLY

Sunapee dawn, low light
Lighthouse bright white on left, dark in west.
Tree trunks, moored sailboat, everything lit.
A rock island supports a motionless merganser.
The still water is contemplative, reflective.
No birds sing.

I hate to be the one to launch this suspended
      dawn into active day.
I wait while the light heightens behind the pines
More rays pierce the branches:
Lighthouse and little boat slightly less mellow
      in the rising light,
Merganser motionless still.

Attempting an unobtrusive merger, I lower into the
    water.
It gurgles and curls around my body
The quietest swimming is the slowest breast stroke.
Yet the surface rings and rolls and ripples.

The brightness jumps above the tree line,
A dazzling aura, a skied, deified van Gogh
    chrysanthemum.
It has begun.
I turn away from the blinding.

The merganser swims away (now clearly her head is
    red)
        with five ducklings paddling after her.
On signal, swallows come to snatch snacks on the fly.
A wood thrush sings the song of songs.
A newborn breeze ruffles the distance,
Travels, fills, darkens the surface water.
Little Folly bobs at her mooring.
The lighthouse is what it is.

One more summer morning is launched.

BATS IN THE BELFRY

I have frequently had bats in my belfry
In the figurative sense
So I was not surprised to see
Swallows in my boathouse
In the literal sense.

Flying furious at my head
They told me I was cheap, cheap, cheap.
I felt my Audubon belt slipping.
Who did they think they were:
Nesting in my rafters
And excreting on my boat and bathing suit?

After a few days their fierce defenses
Softened to a nervous toleration.
They seemed to have agreed among themselves
To share my boathouse with me.
My boat was still targeted
But my purple bathing suit they kept in violet.

A few days more and they treated me
As though I were invisible,
Which, far from giving me hopes of Franciscan
    friendships to come,
Rather hurt my feelings.

I put on my suit every morning and evening of the
   summer
Eased into the lake and swam my swims.
As I swam I could see
Swallows, one after another, hurtling out of the door
Like broncos from the chute
Swinging up and out, seriously intent.

They sang, you won't believe it,
Alexander's Ragtime Band!
"Come on and hear; come on and hear"
As they flew their singular swallow flight:
A flurry of wing beats to get up to speed,
A lift that lasts to the edge of a fall
Which, at the ultimate moment before debacle,
Is saved by a new flurry of wing beats.

Keats spoke, in words that stick,
Of swallows twittering in the sky.
Boathouse swallows twitter
When daylight softens until
Clear outlines change to impressionisms
And impressions to memories.
Insects come humming, not knowing
Whose protein they are soon to be.
The swallows swing out over the lake
Trusting their nests and their nestlings
To me.

HAMPSHIRE—THE HILL

By summer's end I knew every rock on this path.
Could go in the dark by Braille
Through the woods
From the cottage winding   far   down to the lake.

When I first got here
I could remember only the major smooth stepping
    stones.
A week of stubbing bleeding great toes
And I had mastered the minor jutting obstacles.

Then the joy of insouciant speed
Up and down that rock-infested hill.
One misstep could cost me blood and unmatched
    pain;
Yet I never made that miss.

I could feel the warm round stones
As the hollow of my foot recognized them,
Imagine the rough rocks as my feet passed
In thoughtlesss avoidance.

I remember myself on "pardine sallies"
(I got that out of an English novel),
Surefooted, smooth, sliding through the
Dappled shade by day,
Or the dappled moonlight by some nights,
Or the utter blind black night on others,
Where I went easily in the dark by Braille.

As leopards do.

RACING THE RAIN TO THE RASPBERRIES

I took the old blue colander with me
    down the dirt road
While leaves turned inside out
Signalling the coming rain that I could smell.
The thunder sounded cranky in the distance.

The red raspberries were perfectly ripe
Red among prickly leaves high as my breast.
I pulled the berries gently off their pith
(the handle that holds them on the bush).
They looked like salmon roe accumulating in
    the colander.

About then the mosquitos found me.
Oh for lovers as ardent!
I tried to maintain a monomaniacal concentration
Despite their high narrow song of intention,
although it is hard to ignore the
insistent attentions of a vampire mosquito.

A few big drops of rain the size of my watch,
A crack of close thunder brought a new wind
That caused birch and popple-leaves to show
    their silver sides more menacingly.

A snake trickled down the slope among the bushes.
My sweat turned cold.
My back hairs rose.
My feet said, "Quick let's go."
But I made them stay for just one more bush
Loaded with ripeness and smelling like summer
(Is it getting dark?).
Once I had that, another, deeper in, lured me
     scratched me, mosquitoed me.
And another and another
(Yes, it is getting dark).

I walked out of the resisting bramble bushes.
They pulled my shirt, my pants.
They sharply tried to hold back my brown summer
  skin.

I ran home as smoothly as the snake
so no bouncing berries would escape.

Bam! A really big crash.
The rain hurled itself down, angry for some reason
    of its own.
I thought of the berries I'd missed being knocked
    to the ground.

I was inside; the screen door slammed an echoing
    bam.
My epidermis was a tingle, each sting discrete and
        poignant.
My pants were stained and my shirt was torn.

I looked at the comfortable clusters of hairy berries,
some still evoking the blossom that bore them.
I saw a green bug, the size of this comma,.
He had two radio-telephone antennae on his rear
and two ordinary antennae on his front.
And there was a dark brown insect equally small
with a curious cross on his carapace.
Gently I lifted them.

When the rain is through, I thought, I will put them
    back on the bush.
Meanwhile they can rest in the ramekin of moss I
    keep on my table.

These are the first, maybe the last, and only wild
        raspberries of my summer.
I have no regrets.
I braved the mosquitos and raced the rain, because
These berries are my gift of love for your birthday.

SIXISH ON SUMMER MORNINGS

Sixish on summer mornings
It feels so airy
Walking down to the lake
    in your own body.
The sleepy breeze and the young sun
    are negligent.

You walk right into the water.
When submerged, your surface seems the smoothest
    and softest of materials
When you walk out of the water,
Into the arms of a rough blue towel,
You are drying the toughest of materials.

Climbing back up the hill, the curious wind and
    the wide-eyed sun find you,
Remind you its time to add
    cotton and leather and a public face.

HEATHER'S LAST SWIM

Today, after a long hiatus,
She swims with me
Indian style
Hardly rippling the water before her chest,
Ears afloat, whiskers erect, tail streaming out behind.

Side by side we glide
Not far from shore,
Smelling the pitch from the new cut pine,
Hearing the Kingfisher rattle,
Feeling the soft water return our limber youth.

Sometimes she circles me
And I touch her lightly
Or let her pretend to tow me with her tail.

We continue our matched pace, harmonious, easy.
I wonder if we swim too far and if she, so old,
May die from this impulsive reminiscent effort
But it is a good way and a good day to die:
A day that is warm and clear,
A day of return to the soft water
Bathing in the immutable intimacy
A dog and her girl.

DOG DONE SWIMMING

Dog done swimming
Does a classical four dimensional shake.
She walks away
Leaving her impressionistic painting on the
       weathered wooden deck.

LAST DAY IN HAMPSHIRE—SEPTEMBER 1984

The sky is still cranky,
Even after raining all day.
The wind is exhausted,
But little whirls of mist rise from the lake,
Tiny storms moving over the liquid desert;
Toothless baby tornadoes,
Helpless infant typhoons.
In our dark craft,
We are alone in a mythical illustration
Where Ulysses and Jason have drifted.

COLUMBUS AVENUE PASTURE

A field of snow is shaped with a black line of
    barbed wire,
Now no place for daisies or mallows to bloom among
    grasses.
Back to the wind, the stolid work horse endures the
    winter.
He is sniffing, unappetized by the pile of dark hay
    that has been pitched to him.
As fully formed as a Rubens nude,
This horse looks strong in his heavy weather furs:
Sway-backed, round-bellied, ruffled on his hocks,
And lovely long disheveled mane the color of milk.
Providentially, in my pocket, hang seven brown sugar
    lumps
(saved from my teas on a Cornwall vacation).
Though the light is failing, the great horse sees the
    platter, my proffered hand.
His curious eye gleams in the dusk.
He whickers. He nibbles, exploring for my gift.
And I feel the thrilling softness of his lips.
He nods, up and down, experiencing the new feel
    and flavor of sugar.

"Merry Christmas", I wish him,
While I pat his neck vigorously so he'll feel me
   through his coat,
         through the muffled sound.

Long time we stand face to face in the dark in the
   snow.
I smell the memory of last summer's flowers on his
   breath.

SAILING

THINGS THAT GO BUMP IN THE NIGHT
(Brasdor Lake—August 27, 1983)

Something woke me, bumping in the night.
Seven bells. I figure three-thirty.
I took my flashlight and went up on deck,
Dew wet on my bare feet.
Mother of pearl clouds were back-lit by the moon.
The wind blew up the tail of my nightgown
Lightly feathering my nether regions.

Resisting the sensuality of the night
I flashed the light:
The dinghy was on too short a tether.
She was pitching and nudging her mother ship.
Merlin slept on.
I told her to hush,
Loosened her line, recleated it and tied a safety
    bowline on the rail.
Turning to go below
I glanced sideways, a farewell peek at the sky light.
Synchronously, impulsively, the moon exposed herself
        fully to me.
I smiled shyly, stepped below,
Slipped and zipped into my sleeping bag
And slid to oblivion.

LOUSE HARBOR III

The smooth grey granite shore
Was transmogrified
Into an old bent bearded man,
A charging buffalo with lichen on his back,
Silver fishes arching, a tuna perhaps,
A fallen totem pole,
An elephant listening,
A half submerged hippopotamus,
Seals sliding in and out of the sea,
And pillows and cushions of deep and downy stone.

Resting on the softest of these
Was one of the minor pharoahs
Arms crossed, a recumbent Osiris,
Wrapped in fair linen
His binding carelessly unfinished
As if the funerary priests
Had just that moment gone to lunch.

THE SEA OFF NEWFOUNDLAND
(August 1984)

On the edges of Newfoundland the sea is
Ironed, smooth, reflective,
Tessellated, chunky, geological.

That water can be
Blue, black, white,
Or breaking, bottle-green, over your bow and your
  body.

It can be
Warm, cold,
Soft hard,
Clean, dirty,
Life-giving, life-taking,
Cheerful, gloomy, motherly, school-masterly,
Romantic, erotic, mythical, melancholy,
Luminous, numinous,
Friendly,
Indifferent,
Pitiless,
Unforgiving,
Ferocious,
Final.

CINQ CERFS TO ACONITE

Our ship is small
In the exact center
Of a blue plate
Whose outer edge is a clear clean line.

Storm petrels surf beside us
Just long enough to see who we are.

We sail and sail
Never leaving our position
In the very center of the plate,
No danger of falling off the edge.

And on and on and on.
Arching down the hemisphere of the sky,
The sun lies at last on the edge of the dish,
No longer to be looked at except askance.
Red.
Afterglow.
Mauve softens above the sharp   circumference.

The sky
Which all day displayed a manly blue
Now becomes feminine, even French,
While wisps of wind clouds go pink.

The Eastern side of our circle darkens;
The Western side also,
Except for an alley of brilliance from our boat to the
   edge where the sun slid down.
Night does not fall.
It is simply there.

PHOSPHORESCENTS

In darkest night
Bumbling to the head
And pumping water in
Appears
A circle of phosphorescents
A dome of constellations
Marine and luminous
Profoundly numinous.
I bumble back to bed
To muse on cosmic things.

BRAS D'OR LAKES
(Août 1984)

Two tall bald
Teetering on top
Highest greenest spike,
Beak to beak
They pipe,
Not caring who hears.
Is it an argument?
A duet?
A conversation between the deaf?
Why should they care?
They know we don't speak Eagle.

EAST HAMPTON

LOVE FIFTEEN

Ladies and gentlemen in white clothes
Bash yellow balls about the green and springy lawn.
The long back swing and the fluid follow through
Alternate with awkward emergency effort.

Swallows skim a bare foot above the close mown
    grass
Describing figure eights lying down, the symbol for
    infinity.
The sky is summer blue, infinite in its own
    symbolism.

Picking up balls for the next serve
Along the chain link fence clung with Virginia
    Creeper,
Glimpses of the space beyond   seen and heard:
The high side of a seesaw,
Half a head of yellow curls,
A tan foot in a red sandal,
A partial pot of pink geraniums,
A slant of rope for a swing,
Snatches of a song of someone's self
A shovel gritting on sand
Mother calling from the house.
Love Forty.

EARLY MORNING HOOK POND

Pinkly pleased and delightedly embarrassed,
I heard my father clapping,
For me!
In the school play.
Solo, lento, a cappella, double forte.

Lying in my old bed in my childhood room,
Toes and nose to the morning light,
The sun, as always, shined open my lids.

I could see laid out on a sun ray
The lifetime since we girls
Wrote, directed, produced, performed The Hilaria.
Then I understood
That I have no father,
And had none even then when
We gave that show for the whole school,
And for our parents.

And I saw through the window
That my endearing applause
Came, not from my dream,
But from a male mute swan
Whacking the water with his wide wings,
Determined to be airborne:
Solo, lento, a cappella, double forte.

EAST HAMPTON GALE 1984

In a forty knot gale a Herring gull
Fishes to windward in the curls of successive tall
    storm waves
Which build and rise
Until
Their equilibrium
Tips.
Then they roll, slide, skid down themselves
In a thunder of white confusion.
The wind hurls back the arch of their fall,
Hurls it high in the air
Thicker than smoke,
Thinner than water.
Now the gull flies straight up
To get away from it all.
Empty beak and belly
Impel him to turn again to windward
Tucked tight into   the next curl of impending ocean.

THE FALL

A scorching day ends in aerobic dusk.
Up the dark walnut trunks, cathedral high,
The arching leaves permit twilight only in the vault.
Out of which a bat circles, blindly, blackly,
    indistinctly,
He slowly spirals down to light on the gravel drive.
His landing is unexpectedly crisp!
Correction:
That was the absolute first autumn leaf to fall.

MAINE

ORR ISLAND AILES DE DEUX

When they do mohawks and double axles
Swan dives or half gainers
Telemarks or christies
In musical rhythmic pairs
The slower it goes
The more difficult, dangerous, and
The more achingly sweet it is.
Yet no human pas de deux
Can come close
To this pair of osprey above
Orr Island.

I, ungainly, could not aspire
To even human
Outer immelmens
Or inner outermens
On a cold, bright Maine morning.

They, not fishing,
Are just coasting on the breeze,
Together
Carving their ins and outs
Overs and unders
With clear-cut grace.

Meanwhile their big nest-bound child
With a great pathetic sense
And no aesthetic sense
Cries for fish to fill his belly.

Rather should he
Admire (and envy)
His parents' lovely lyric
Expressed in slow winged daring.
Admire
So much
That he takes
That
Fateful
Possibly plummeting
Step into the
Air
And is
Off.
Beating and up!
On his own
To fish and find a partnership
As arch and wheeling
And easy
As this
Pair of osprey
Now.
Above Orr Island.

NEW HAY

When I walk by
New hay
Hosses
And manua
I hear
Freddy Witcher
Say
Shuwa
Though that be,
I dern well know
Fotty mebbee fotty-one
Fotty-two
Years ago.

SKYWATCH

Walk out on that high cliff at low tide
And lie on your back on the warm flat top.
High raveling clouds are moving out to sea
Blowing by the still empyrean   blue sky.
You get a sense of falling up
Dangerous but not really frightening.
There's a gull flying across the cloud
Straight above, flying into the wind
So that he glides and needs no wing flap to stay aloft
(Very understandable, because neither do you).
Under a passed cloud the sun is released
And gilds the tail and trailing edges of the
Gull's gliding wings:
A sudden brilliance that catches the lofted mind
And is gone.
Then you are regular old you again, lying on your
  back on
    flat rock,
And the sea pushing and pulling far below
Reminds you of the gravity of the situation.

A COLD DAY IN NOVEMBER

Two red flags on the lighthouse yardarm
Announced a gale which piled up clouds in the
    southwest.
The low late afternoon sun shot through a hole,
Silvered the edge of the horizon where the sea ends
And the tops of the grey waves
In three long diagonals of shine.

You weren't there, so you won't believe it,
But even if you were, you would have been dazzled.
Seeing the dull sea set off with silver,
You would shiver and look again to be sure you saw.
And look again to remember the work of November's
    smiths.

BAHAMAS

TEMPORARY AQUATIC
PHILOGENETIC REGRESSION

My long body is resting face down in the sea.
The sand below is overlayed with moving nets of
    golden light, which,
From time to time, break into rainbows of silent
    laughter.

I undulate over savannahs of grass no taller than my
    hand,
Waving in their own undersea breezes.
I drift into a cloud of silver minnows.
No, not silver: they have pale yellow and semi-
            perceptible blue stripes along them
A moving metropolis, a cast of thousands,
Their dominant edges lead the shimmering pointilist
    city.
When they see large, floating, glass-faced,
    fin-footed me,
They turn abruptly, en masse, away.

I lie dissolving in the soft bed of water
The population of fishes turns again and parts,
            flowing around, incorporating me.

I move with them, toes only.

Who's in charge here?

The outer edge of minnows steers
Until a slight shift makes them inner minnows.
Still ensemble, we swim on, keeping our individual
    distances with infinite care.
Inexplicably, in the blink of an eye, my fellow fish
    scoot away without me.

They know what I am not fish enough to feel.
I see what they knew: a barracuda hanging in the
    water.
He is almost my size with a mouthful of teeth.
I see his black eye.
His black eye sees me.
Curious? Hungry?
My outer edges scoot for shore in full fright
Breathless, thrashing, I imagine his implacable
    approach.
A lifetime later, I roll onto the sand, pull off
        my mask and fins,
Breathe the free air and laugh out loud
For the joy of being a woman again.

NEW YORK CITY

SMILES

Smiles are serious business.
Perhaps thought-worthy.
You decide.
I show you my teeth.
You show me yours.
Maybe we have exchanged smiles of peace.
The young dog bellies up,
The wolf offers his throat,
In short form, we forego making head and hand
   vulnerable;
We just smile.
That says I won't hurt you,
Please don't hurt me.
Or maybe we have smiled a smile of recognition.
I see someone I know,
I automatically give the recognition smile.
I see you
And
Depending on the day,
Give a shy smile with downcast eye
That it may not seem unseemly;
But, if all is clear,
I give
The wide open, the broad, the truly glad
Or maybe the misty smile:
You, whom I love
Have done something so good so fair
That my smile is tear-trembled.

Or the private smile:
That is just to say
We know and they don't.
Or the leer:
There's no mistaking
The threatening implication:
I'm gonna getcha
And that's that.
Or the rueful smile:
That is the punctuation
On the sad observation
That it was ever thus
(And anyhow better than crying).
Or the smile of angst
Which gets no answer:
Doesn't the anguished grimace borrow the smile's
    muscles?
I only know when I do that it hurts so much.
Then there is the selfish smile
That neither intends nor sends messages.
I smile it to myself
When I am strutting along,
Alone
And feeling fine.
I frequently smile
For all these reasons
And sometimes
Just because I want to show off my big white
    beautiful
Teeth.

AFTER TRISTAN

A sleeping violin
Smooth curving in the case, awakes
Hears the footsteps of the maestro,
Sees the light as he opens on the shining,
Feels the lift, the tension of tuning,
And the glorious release of
The arching lines of
The geometric progression of
The legato tenderness of
Itself singing *The Liebestod*.

ON READING
WALT WHITMAN, THE MAKING OF A POET
BY PAUL ZWEIG

Intense,wild,risky,white-heated,
Caressing,tender,melting,sentimental,
Limber,nimble,graceful,
Athletic,muscular,rough-hewn,robust,
Loafing,indolent,easy-going,nonchalant,
Emancipated,exulting,free,ante-intellectual,uncivilized,
Angry,proud,touchy,anarchic,boisterous,brawling,
    untamed,untamable,
Chaotic,turbulent,stormy,windy,violent,dangerous,
Copious,profuse,ample,biblical,evangelical,spacious,
        all-encompassing,abundant,cosmic,
Ambiguous,paradoxical,restless,contradictory,
    wayward,
Epithalamial,rhythmical,rhapsodical,singing-shouting,
        barbarically yawping,musical,
High-handed,posturing,lofty,grandiose,swaggering,
Extravagant,inflated,egotistical,vain,show-offish,
        hortatory,intrusive,

Homely,colloquial,common,democratic,enmasse,
    prosaic,unvarnished,
Dazzling,dramatic,stagey,actory,
Stupendous,vivid,luxuriant,effervescent,flamboyant,
    fluorescent,
Gay,antic,prancing,buoyant,arm-flapping,
Flirtatious,spontaneous,adventurous,manic,
Physical,naked,lusty,hot,ripe,urgent,potent,bursting,
Tantalizing,Greek,animal-spirited,full-blooded,
Erotic,swooning,homosexual,heterosexual,sexual,
    sexual,
Uniting,merging,insatiable,omnivorous,
Original,solitary,innocent,unread,inexperienced,
Poetic,consuming,soaring,unconsummated
Inward,
Indirect,
W. W..

DÉJÀ WHO?

A thrush flew through my thinking place.
I felt the feathers brush my brain,
But it was so swift.
I can't remember.
I can't remember.

POTSDAM

POTSDAM IN OCTOBER

Funny light.
Glaring puddles reflect bright where no sun is
Because there has been rain.
The autumn reds and yellows are extravagant.
The fields are extra green.
The blacks and whites of Holsteins are extra clear.

Funny light.
A trembling V of geese tries the emotional sky.
Grey clouds are stirred in the distance,
Wind-worried and frazzled.
Doughy, indigestible dumplings are overhead,
Heavy but moving through the color of the sky.
A sunburst spots a small green field,
A single beam shines on a spinney of pines,
Straight up is a deep hole
With circular folds spiraling endlessly in.
The passionate sun glares out,
An immaculate conception.

Funny light.
A balloonist in his basket is skudding
Atilt above the treetops,
Scrawling a sassy gaiety across the uncertain sky.
The sky is inscrutable,
Refusing to tell whether the weather

Impends
A teasing excitation,
A religious ecstasy,
Or some sudden, perverse malice.

DATE DUE
